CALIFORNIA
MISSIONS

Discovering Mission San Diego de Alcalá

BY SAM HAMILTON

Cavendish
Square
New York

Published in 2015 by Cavendish Square Publishing, LLC
243 5th Avenue, Suite 136, New York, NY 10016

Website: cavendishsq.com

This publication represents the opinions and views of the author based on his or her personal experience, knowledge, and
research. The information in this book serves as a general guide only. The author and publisher have used their best efforts in
preparing this book and disclaim liability rising directly or indirectly from the use and application of this book.

CPSIA Compliance Information: Batch #WS14CSQ

All websites were available and accurate when this book was sent to press.

Library of Congress Cataloging-in-Publication Data

Hamilton, Sam.
Discovering Mission San Diego de Alcalá / Sam Hamilton.
pages cm. — (California missions)
Includes index.
ISBN 978-1-62713-109-4 (hardcover) ISBN 978-1-62713-111-7 (ebook)
1. San Diego Mission—History—Juvenile literature. 2. Spanish mission buildings—California—San Diego—History—Juvenile
literature. 3. Franciscans—California—San Diego—History—Juvenile literature. 4. California—History—To 1846—Juvenile literature. 5. Kamia Indians—Missions—California—San Diego—History—Juvenile literature. 6. California—History—To 1846—Juvenile
literature. I. Title.
F869.S22H35 2015
979.4'985—dc23
2014008644

Editorial Director: Dean Miller
Editor: Kristen Susienka
Copy Editor: Cynthia Roby
Art Director: Jeffrey Talbot
Designer: Douglas Brooks
Photo Researcher: J8 Media
Production Manager: Jennifer Ryder-Talbot
Production Editor: David McNamara

The photographs in this book are used by permission and through the courtesy of: Cover photo by julius fekete/Shutterstock.com;
Stock Connection/SuperStock, 1; Richard Cummins/Robert Harding World Imagery/Getty Images, 4; Kanan H. Jani/File:Juan
Rodriguez Cabrillo at Cabrillo National Monument.jpg/Wikimedia Commons, 6; Edward S. Curtis/File:Edward S. Curtis Collection
People 074.jpg/Wikimedia Commons, 8; Durova/File:Kumeyaai basket.jpg/Wikimedia Commons, 9; Courtesy of UC Berkeley,
Bancroft Library, 10; © 2014 Pentacle Press, 13; RES Photo Services, 14; Photo courtesy of www.virginstamps.com, 16; © Pentacle
Press, 18; omer sukru goksu/E+/iStock.com, 21; © Pentacle Press, 22; RES Photo Services, 25; akg-images/Joseph Martin/Newscom,
26; © Pentacle Press, 29; RES Photo Services, 30; Alex Covarrubias/File:Flag of Mexico.svg/Wikimedia Commons, 31; Courtesy
of UC Berkeley, Bancroft Library, 32–33; Mdhennessey/File:SD restored property.png/Wikimedia Commons, 33; David Madison/
Photographer's Choice/Getty Images, 34; RES Photo Services, 36; julius fekete/Shutterstock.com, 41.

Printed in the United States of America

Contents

Mission San Diego de Alcalá, started in 1769,
was the first mission in Alta California.

1
The Spanish Explore San Diego

High on a hill, about 5 miles (8 kilometers) from the Pacific Ocean in the city of San Diego, lies Mission San Diego de Alcalá, the first of twenty-one Spanish missions built along California's coast. On arrival, visitors can see the church, the bell tower, and the white walls surrounding the mission's interior. This is a place filled with history told by the men, women, and children who lived there.

EXPLORING THE NEW WORLD

Spain's interest in this part of the world began after Christopher Columbus, an Italian explorer working for Spain's king and queen, returned from a sea voyage in 1493. He had been searching for a direct water route from Europe to Asia and had accidentally discovered a new world (North America, South America, and Central America) full of riches, people, and land. Spain, in search of gold and spices, was eager to explore this new area. The country also hoped to settle the land and **convert** the Native people to the most dominant religion at that time: Catholicism. In the years following Columbus's journey, Spain sent explorers and soldiers to find out all they could about the land.

The first explorer following Columbus's route was Hernán

Juan Rodríguez Cabrillo, honored with a monument in California, made detailed maps of the area.

Cortés. In 1519, Cortés and his men sailed to what is now known as Mexico. There they encountered a large Native group called the Aztecs, whom they defeated in 1521. Cortés then claimed the Aztec's land for Spain and renamed the area New Spain.

In 1542, Juan Rodríguez Cabrillo was sent on a voyage to explore the west coast of North America. Up until then, Europeans believed California was an island. Cabrillo's detailed maps would change the way Europeans viewed that part of the world. Also at that time, the name "Californias" described the land that is now the state of California and the peninsula known today as the Baja Peninsula of Mexico. The state of California was then called *Alta*, or upper, California, while the Baja Peninsula was known as *Baja*, or lower, California.

The last of the early explorers to visit California was Sebastián Vizcaíno. He and his men sailed in 1602, searching for a way to connect the Atlantic and Pacific Oceans. While there, they founded the cities of San Diego (previously named San Miguel by Cabrillo) and Monterey. However, since their journey did not lead to discovering a water route or desired riches, Spain decided not to send any more people there. One hundred sixty years would pass before more Spanish explorers would come to California.

2
The
Kumeyaay

Before the Spanish came to settle Alta California in the 1760s, the land's Native population was large and diverse. Because there are no written records, no one knows when the first Native people arrived in the area. It is estimated that around 20,000 years ago, people crossed a bridge of land between Alaska and Russia and gradually settled in small groups, called tribes, all along California's coast. Each group had its own language and beliefs. Several villages could belong to the same tribe, and in each village there was a leader, called a chief.

The Native group living near the San Diego area was known as the Kumeyaay. They lived in villages near the ocean or the San Diego River.

KUMEYAAY WAY OF LIFE

Little is known about the Kumeyaay prior to the Spanish arriving in the area. Historians have examined artifacts and records written by Spanish explorers to understand how the group lived and operated.

According to historians, the Kumeyaay were resourceful people, living off the land and making tools and weapons, and building homes from the resources in their environment. Using bark, brush, and grass they built *ewaas*, or dome-shaped houses. Each ewaa likely had its own fire pit and a hole in its roof so the fire's smoke could escape. Weapons such as spears, arrowheads, and snares were made from wood, stone, flint, and obsidian.

The Kumeyaay were a nomadic people, meaning they moved from place to place to find food during the different seasons. They had the freedom to live life as they pleased. Each village had a specific winter and summer location to which they migrated when the weather changed. They lived close to the land, remaining near

Kumeyaay houses, called eewas, were created from brush and branches. Here a Kumeyaay woman sits in front of her traditional house.

The Kumeyaay wove intricate baskets with unique designs. Some of these baskets are on display at the Museum of Man in San Diego.

areas abundant in sources of natural foods. Over time they also developed harvesting techniques that were passed on from generation to generation. They would know when to harvest plants and at which time in a plant's life to do it.

The men were hunters and fishermen. They used many different handmade tools to hunt food such as rabbit, deer, duck, fish, and clams. The most important staple food was the acorn. Acorns could be stored for long periods of time and ground to make flour for breads and other food.

The Kumeyaay were also skilled in making tightly woven baskets. Women usually made them, and they were used for food storage, cooking, and carrying water. These baskets were also used as women's hats.

CLOTHING

In the warm Alta California climate, the men wore little or no clothing. In cooler weather, they draped animal **hides** over their shoulders for warmth. Women wore skirts fashioned of willow

Known to the early Spanish settlers as the Diegueno tribe, the Kumeyaay (depicted in this illustration from a 1857 U.S.-Mexico boundary survey) saw significant changes to their culture due to their interactions with the missions.

bark or reeds. Both men and women wore their hair long. Some wore necklaces made of shells or armbands made of twisted hair. Women often painted their faces and bodies.

COMMUNICATION

The Kumeyaay had extensive communication routes between villages and within their own territories. This made it easy to get information from one place to another. Each tribe had messengers, called runners, who would deliver messages quickly when needed. This communication system helped alert people in the early days of the Alta California missions.

RELIGIOUS BELIEFS AND PRACTICES

The natural world was important to the Kumeyaay. They respected people, the land, and all of Earth's creatures. They believed in many gods and spirits. Some gods influenced the natural world, while others impacted human life. The Kumeyaay relied on healers, called shamans, to treat the sick. It was believed that these men and women could heal people by dancing, singing, and using herbs and other remedies.

Ceremonies were a common part of the Kumeyaay culture. **Rituals** were held to honor births, weddings, wars, hunting trips, and the dead. Both boys and girls took part in initiation ceremonies to enter adulthood. Dancing and singing were important parts of these ceremonies.

All of this changed, though, when the Spanish arrived to build Mission San Diego de Alcalá.

3
The Mission System

More than 200 years before the Spanish encountered the Kumeyaay, they began colonizing the New World. The first area to be colonized was New Spain, or what is known today as Mexico. There soldiers, settlers, and religious leaders established Mexico City as their capital. Other smaller cities were built throughout New Spain, and it was not long before religious communities, called missions, were also created.

THE FIRST MISSIONS

In the 1600s, Spain wanted to change the way they dealt with Native people around them. Previously, the Spanish had treated the Native people badly and started many wars with various groups. Over time they decided it was better to try and get along peacefully with the Native people, so they brought *frays*—the Spanish word meaning friars—from Spain to Baja California to create missions in the area. Their goal was to convert the Native people to Christianity and have them learn Spanish traditions, customs, and religious beliefs. After accepting Christianity, the Native people would learn to live like the Spanish, thus becoming Spanish citizens. This increase in population would help the

Spanish empire expand. It was thought that after about ten years, the missions would be handed over to the Native people to manage. However, this never happened.

The Spanish empire was growing steadily. Many missions were built in New Spain, all run by friars. Then in the mid-1700s, the Spanish king, Carlos III, heard that Russian and English troops were building forts in Alta California. This worried him because he wanted all of California to belong to Spain. It was then decided to send groups of soldiers and priests into Alta California to build a chain of missions and *presidios*, or forts, to expand Spain's rule.

The person to lead these missions was a promising missionary

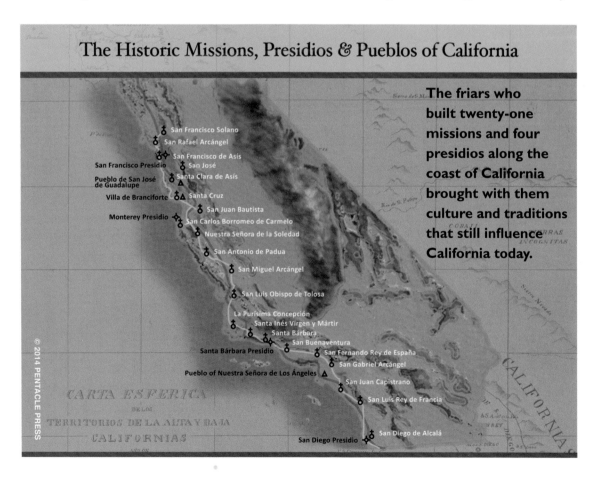

The Historic Missions, Presidios & Pueblos of California

The friars who built twenty-one missions and four presidios along the coast of California brought with them culture and traditions that still influence California today.

San Francisco Solano
San Rafael Arcángel
San Francisco de Asís
San Francisco Presidio
San José
Pueblo de San José de Guadalupe
Santa Clara de Asís
Villa de Branciforte
Santa Cruz
San Juan Bautista
Monterey Presidio
San Carlos Borromeo de Carmelo
Nuestra Señora de la Soledad
San Antonio de Padua
San Miguel Arcángel
San Luis Obispo de Tolosa
La Purísima Concepción
Santa Inés Virgen y Mártir
Santa Bárbara
San Buenaventura
Santa Bárbara Presidio
San Fernando Rey de España
San Gabriel Arcángel
Pueblo of Nuestra Señora de Los Ángeles
San Juan Capistrano
San Luis Rey de Francia
San Diego de Alcalá
San Diego Presidio

© 2014 PENTACLE PRESS

13

from Majorca, Spain: fifty-five-year-old Fray Junípero Serra. Fray Serra had experienced much success converting Native people and leading the Baja California missions. It was this experience that led to Fray Serra being chosen as the founding president of the Alta California missions. He was also tasked to discover the perfect places to construct mission sites, and thereby ventured north into Alta California with explorer and soldier Captain Gaspár de Portolá to found the first mission, San Diego de Alcalá, in 1769.

Fray Junípero Serra led an expedition to found Mission San Diego in 1769. He is remembered as the father of the California missions.

4
Founding Mission San Diego de Alcalá

In early 1769, the Spanish government sent five expeditions from New Spain to Alta California to found the first mission and *presidio*, as well as to search for the city of Monterey. Three ships set sail northward along the California coast, while two land expeditions—one led by Fray Serra and Portolá—were sent through the rocky, desert terrain of Baja California. All of the expedition groups were to meet at the harbor in San Diego Bay. The Spanish government had given about $1,000 in Spanish money, or *pesetas*, to the friars joining Fray Serra on this expedition. The money was to purchase supplies for Mission San Diego de Alcalá and bells for the church.

THE JOURNEY NORTH

The journey north was difficult for everyone. When it began, Fray Serra was almost fifty-six years old and had a bad leg from a previous injury. He had never traveled to Alta California and relied on the soldiers for guidance and protection. To worsen matters, the trail through New Spain was dusty, and the sun beat down on the travelers. There was a constant worry of attack from the Native groups in the area, who Serra and the others with him feared would

Gaspár de Portolá was a soldier and explorer. Today he is remembered in this Spanish stamp.

be angry that foreigners were entering their territory. The soldiers wore jackets made from leather to protect them from arrows. However, during their journey, Fray Serra and Portolá faced little opposition from the Native groups.

Portolá and Serra's expedition arrived at the harbor of San Diego Bay on July 1, 1769. Two of the ships had already arrived, while another, the *San José*, had been lost at sea. Of the 226 sailors who left New Spain, only half made it to California alive. Many became ill or died from scurvy, a disease caused by a diet lacking fresh fruits and vegetables containing vitamin C.

FOUNDING THE MISSION

As soon as the expedition arrived, Fray Serra knew the area was the right place to build the first mission. Nearby was a hill, later named Presidio Hill, overlooking San Diego Bay. The area was also close to a Kumeyaay village. According to Fray Serra's records, the Native people at first treated the newcomers with "good will."

The men who were well enough to work began building a temporary chapel and other dwellings on the hilltop. They gathered brush in the area and used it to form shelters. The Spanish hoped that eventually the Native people would help them construct sturdier, permanent buildings once they understood the mission was there to stay.

Fray Serra named the mission San Diego, following a Spanish custom of naming the mission after the saint whose **feast day** was closest to the date of their arrival. The missionaries made an altar—a table used to give offerings to God. On July 16, 1769, Fray Serra conducted Mass, a Catholic Church service, and dedicated Mission San Diego de Alcalá to God and to the Spanish empire. This was the first European settlement in southern California.

INVOLVING THE KUMEYAAY

Relations with the Kumeyaay developed slowly over time. Initially, the Kumeyaay were curious about the Spanish and the work they were doing on their land. Before long, as construction of the mission began, the Kumeyaay became unhappy. When Fray Serra arrived, many of the men with him were sick and thereby had weakened. This made it easy for the Kumeyaay to observe the travelers and then raid the area. Over the first few weeks of Serra's arrival, the Kumeyaay took sections of the soldiers' ships' sails and rope. They also took goods such as fabrics and tools. They left what little food was there, however, because they thought that it had made the men ill. On August 12, a two-day battle between the Kumeyaay and the Spanish soldiers took place. The Natives' weapons were no match against Spanish guns, and soon the Kumeyaay decided to tolerate the Spanish rather than fight them.

The Spanish had many tools, fabrics, and trinkets that were unfamiliar to the Kumeyaay, and the soldiers and missionaries used these items to attract them to the mission. The Kumeyaay watched as the Spanish quickly cut down trees using metal axes and saws. Some of the Kumeyaay wanted to try these tools, so they offered to help. Once the Native people began to help, the Spanish tried to keep them involved in building the mission and presidio, which was built in 1771. The friars spoke to them about Christianity. Some listened and were baptized, but others refused to have anything to do with the Christian god.

After the temporary shelters were constructed, Fray Serra continued on to Monterey to found the second mission. He left frays Luis Jaymé and Vicente Fustér in charge of building and overseeing the mission's operations in San Diego until he could return.

Many Native men, women, and children helped build the twenty-one missions.

5
Early Days of the Mission

The first five years at Mission San Diego de Alcalá were difficult for the missionaries and soldiers. They needed the help of **neophytes**, or newly converted Native people, to build their structures and to help populate the mission but faced many challenges.

DIFFICULTIES ENCOUNTERED

Many Kumeyaay were reluctant to join the mission system. In the first two years of the mission, no Kumeyaay converted. They did not understand why the Spanish had arrived on their lands and brought with them strange traditions.

In 1771, Fray Jaymé and Fray Fustér decided to go out and seek converts for the mission. They traveled into nearby Native villages and farther inland and spoke to many Native people. This approach upset some of the Native communities. Many tolerated the presence of the foreigners and even traded with them. But what they did not want was to have Christian beliefs forced on them. Another event harmed the friars' attempts even further.

In October 1771, soldiers from the presidio hurt the wife of one of the Native chiefs (called a *Kwai-pai*). The Native people attacked the soldiers, and a few Natives were killed, including the

Kwai-pai. These actions made the Kumeyaay upset and many refused to listen to the priests.

Initially, it was difficult for the friars to communicate with the Kumeyaay. This made it hard to convert the Native people. The more the priests ministered to the Kumeyaay, the angrier the Kumeyaay became. Still, some Kumeyaay believed the friars were powerful shamans and decided to become neophytes. By 1774, there were less than one hundred converts, and for that reason, and because good planting soil and water were difficult to find there, it was decided to move the mission six miles away.

Once the mission site had moved, the priests resumed efforts to convert the Kumeyaay. Between July and September of 1775, more than four hundred Natives were baptized, including those who were leaders. Some historians believe that the increase in the numbers of neophytes was not by will but the Spanish forcing many of the Natives to convert to Christianity.

CONSTRUCTING THE MISSION

At both mission locations, those tasked with the actual construction gathered the materials necessary to make the structures permanent. They collected wood to create a foundation, chopped down many trees, and then cut them into planks and posts to make supports for the buildings. They used *carretas*, or small wooden carts pulled by oxen, to move the lumber to the building site. The mission would be constructed in a square shape called a **quadrangle**. Almost all missions built after Mission San Diego de Alcalá followed this design.

At the mission, permanent structures were built using adobe brick.

Next the workers made **adobe** bricks for the walls. The missionaries showed others—including Kumeyaay women and children—how to mix clay, water, and straw together to make adobe. They packed the mixture into wooden molds. Once the bricks were formed, the molds were removed, and the bricks were left to dry in the sun. The dried bricks were then used to build the walls. Mud was placed between the bricks to hold the wall together. The roofs were made of **thatched** reeds and tree branches. It was not until 1784 that all of the mission buildings were completed.

CONFLICT BREWS

As months passed, many Native Californians continued to resent the way the Spanish treated them. The Spanish soldiers abused them and took their land. Diseases such as smallpox and measles had been brought over by the Europeans and affected the Native people, and the friars tried to change their beliefs. Before long the Kumeyaay decided to fight back. In late 1775, news about a planned revolt spread quickly among the Native population, and it was only a matter of time until they attacked.

In the early morning of November 5, 1775, the Kumeyaay, joined by other Native tribes, stormed the mission. Vestments—special clothing worn in religious ceremonies—and other religious articles were stolen from the church, and fire was set to the mission buildings. Within moments of the fighting, Fray Jaymé was shot down by arrows and beaten. He died from his injuries. A Spanish blacksmith and a carpenter at the mission also died. Since the mission had moved, there were only eleven soldiers living there. Other soldiers at the presidio were farther away and couldn't arrive fast enough to help. When more soldiers did arrive, the fighting had ceased.

When Fray Serra, who was now at Mission San Carlos Borroméo del Río Carmelo, received word of this attack, he wrote to government officials in New Spain pleading for mercy for the Native people involved. Punishing the Natives would slow the friars' progress at the mission. The government in New Spain agreed to Serra's request, but the hostility between the friars and the Kumeyaay continued for several months.

Native people resented how they were being treated at the mission and retaliated against the friars and soldiers, killing Fray Jaymé, who became California's first martyr.

6
Daily Life

When tensions between the Natives and the missionaries eased, rebuilding of the mission began. The roofs were replaced with clay tiles, which could better resist fire. More buildings were created and more neophytes joined. It was not long before the mission began to succeed.

LIVING AT MISSION SAN DIEGO DE ALCALÁ

The soldiers and the friars at Mission San Diego de Alcalá had to adjust to a new environment, a new climate, and the isolation of being away from home and family. Mission life provided few comforts. The dwellings were rustic with earthen floors. Blankets were made of scratchy, coarse wool. The food was often plain.

In the early stages of the mission, the Spanish worked together to clear lands, construct buildings, farm, and tend to the livestock. The soldiers protected the mission and its people from attacks by European settlers and the Kumeyaay.

The friars schooled the neophytes in religion, agriculture, cooking, trades, crafts, and ranching. They often worked alongside their pupils in the fields or workshops. They were also responsible for conducting religious services, weddings, funerals, and baptisms.

The friars maintained detailed records of life at the mission so they could report their progress to the Spanish government. For example, in 1797, they recorded that Mission San Diego de Alcalá had acquired 565 new neophytes, for a total of 1,400. The mission owned 20,000 sheep, 10,000 cattle, and 1,250 horses.

HOUSING

Unlike at the other missions in Alta California, the neophytes at Mission San Diego de Alcalá lived both in their own villages and at the mission but on a rotational basis. This was due to the shortage of food at the mission. Not all neophytes came to the mission to work. Some joined to gain more knowledge, while others genuinely believed in the Christian religion. Whatever their reasons, they all had to help with daily activities.

LIFE FOR THE NEOPHYTES

Mission life was quite different from the lifestyle the Kumeyaay had known prior to the arrival of the Spanish. Most days at the mission began when the bells rang in the *campanario*, or bell tower, around sunrise. The bells signaled that it was time to go to Mass. *Atole*, a mush made of grain or corn, was served for breakfast afterward.

Once breakfast was over, the day's work assignments were given. The men were sent to work in the fields, orchards, or workshops. The Spanish showed the neophyte men how to grow crops such as wheat, beans, corn, barley, grapes, fruit, and vegetables. They also taught them European methods of raising cattle, sheep, horses, mules, and goats. In the workshops, the Kumeyaay learned to make leather goods, metal tools, candles, tiles, and adobe. They also worked to repair the mission and construct new buildings.

Neophyte women made food, baskets, cloth, and soap. The Spanish taught them to cook using brick ovens. Some of the women gathered edible plants and nuts when time allowed. They were also taught to use Spanish looms to weave blankets and clothing for themselves, the neophyte men and children, the soldiers, and the friars.

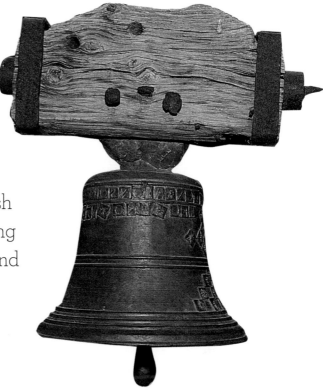

Bells were an important part of mission rituals. This bell was cast in 1894 and is still in use today.

Children also helped at the mission. In the mornings, the friars taught them the Spanish language and Christianity, and in the afternoons, they helped with chores: cleaning and taking care of the animals.

At midday, work stopped for lunch, a meal that consisted of *pozole*—a soup with grain, vegetables, and meat. Lunch was followed by a *siesta*, or rest period, and then work resumed.

In the evening there was supper and prayers. There was a period of relaxation before bedtime. Many neophytes especially liked to use this time for games.

On occasion, *fiestas*, or parties, would break the monotony of routine mission life. Fiestas were held for weddings, births, and other celebrations. The neophytes sometimes held ceremonies that featured traditional dances and songs from their heritage. Many friars allowed these rituals so the neophytes would remain peaceful and continue their instruction in Christianity. Some songs and dances were included in Catholic religious services.

PAINTINGS

While life at the mission continued to both challenge and educate the Kumeyaay who joined, friars continued to convert

José de Páez's paintings illustrated Christian beliefs to the Native people.

others to Christianity. One way of converting them was through art. Fray Serra asked one of his favorite painters, José de Páez, to create realistic scenes from different Bible stories. The artwork depicted heaven, which helped the friars explain their religion to the Natives.

WATER AT THE MISSION

Ample resources of water for the mission were important to the survival of both people and animals there. Following a severe drought in 1800, the friars decided to build an **irrigation system** to deliver water to them. Neophytes and soldiers constructed a dam on the San Diego River. Water was then brought to the mission by way of an **aqueduct**, which carried it five miles. This was a difficult task that took many hours of work. Part of the dam and the aqueduct remains intact today.

7
Troubles and Hardships

Besides maintaining rigorous schedules and working long and tiring hours, the friars, soldiers, and the Kumeyaay neophytes who lived at the mission continued to experience hardships.

PUNISHMENT AND ILLNESS

Many converts, while living at Mission San Diego de Alcalá, suffered for numerous reasons. Friars were concerned that the neophytes would practice their old ways and beliefs if allowed to leave. The neophytes who remained could not return to their villages until it was time for them to do so. The mission's doors were locked at night. If the Kumeyaay tried to escape, the soldiers caught them, brought them back, and sometimes beat them.

Some of the soldiers were very harsh in their treatment of the neophytes. The Spanish had trouble finding men to serve as soldiers in Alta California, so they sent prisoners along with other military men to act as soldiers. Some of these men beat the Native men to death and abused the women. The friars tried to stop the soldiers' abuse. In the 1770s, Fray Serra attempted to ease the soldiers' control over the neophytes by getting written documentation from the government stating that the friars were responsible for the neophytes. This document changed little. Priests too became violent at times and whipped neophytes who did not do their jobs correctly or failed to obey them.

The neophytes lived and worked in cold, damp, and crowded buildings that made breathing difficult. Many of the dormitories had inadequate sanitation systems. The unclean conditions attracted rats and bugs that also brought death and disease to the Kumeyaay. In the early 1800s, a measles epidemic spread throughout the mission system, killing and affecting hundreds of neophytes, who had not developed immunity to these illnesses.

DISASTERS AT THE MISSION

In the years surrounding 1800, there were droughts and then flooding at the mission in San Diego. Crops dried up in the droughts, and nutrients in the soil were washed away in the floods. Both resulted in hunger for the residents of the mission.

In 1803, an earthquake struck the mission, damaging the church. Repairs were made, but in 1808, another earthquake destroyed the work that had been done. Finally, in 1813, a new church was designed to withstand an earthquake. The builders strengthened the walls with buttresses, or extra supports.

ATTACKS ON PRIESTS AND SETTLERS

By 1811 there were many neophytes working and living at Mission San Diego de Alcalá and at the presidio, which was home to soldiers and civilian settlers. All had different roles. Some neophytes served as laborers, participated in church matters, and

Soldiers were harsh in their treatment of the neophytes. This soldier was excommunicated from the church for defying the friars and removing a neophyte.

others oversaw fellow neophytes. One man in particular, Nazario, a cook, became well known for poisoning a mission priest. On November 16, 1811, Nazario was angry and hurt after a friar, Fray José Pedro Panto, had beaten him many times over several days. Seeking revenge, Nazario placed poisonous herbs into the friar's soup, which made the friar very ill. Fray Panto lived, but was upset that Nazario, a man who he trusted, had done this to him. Nazario was put on trial and imprisoned in the presidio for eight months. Others who sought to harm people at the mission and presidio were not so lucky.

In the 1820s, some local Native people who did not live at the mission were frequently raiding its stables for horses. Without horses, it was difficult for those living at the mission to herd the other animals. Many cattle and sheep then wandered away.

Neophytes, friars, and soldiers are buried at Mission San Diego.

In 1826, more conflict arose at the presidio. By this time New Spain, renamed Mexico, had won its independence from Spain and took control over Alta California. This also meant that soldiers who fought in the Mexican War of Independence were gifted large plots of land throughout the region as rewards for their service. This land belonged to the Native people, who were angered because soldiers were moving onto their territory. In that year, Mexican soldiers stationed at the presidio fought a number of small battles, called skirmishes, against the Kumeyaay Native tribes, killing twenty-eight people. Conflict was largely due to difficulties between the Mexican government and the Native population. Similar tensions continued between missionaries, soldiers, and Native people, as well as between Native people and settlers who were living in *ranchos* and the presidio nearby. Over time the conflicts shaped the people living in San Diego, but a greater struggle would spark more unrest when the mission system itself was given over to the Mexican government in 1834.

8
Secularization

After the Mexican government gained control over Alta California, a plan different from that devised by the Spanish was put in place to divide the land. Some Mexicans thought the Native people were being treated like slaves and deserved their freedom and their territories to manage. Others eyed the richness of the mission lands and, out of greed, wanted to take them over.

SECULARIZATION

In the 1830s, the Mexican government decided to secularize the missions by giving them to the Native people. Originally the Spanish intended to secularize the missions themselves after ten years of operation, but the friars had not done this because they believed that the neophytes were not ready to take over the responsibility of running the missions. In August 1834, secularization laws went into effect in California, distributing

Mexico became its own country in 1821 and took over the mission lands.

the mission lands, buildings, and livestock to the neophytes, who were considered free citizens of the new government. However, by that time many Native people had left Mission San Diego de

Alcalá to find work elsewhere or to return to their villages. Only a few friars remained at the missions while many Franciscan friars returned to Spain.

It took nearly fifteen years to release all of the missions in Alta California from the control of the Catholic Church. Most of the mission lands never fell into the hands of the Native people who remained at the missions. Local landowners took the lands for themselves or bought them from corrupt Mexican officials. Some land was gifted to friends of Mexican authorities.

Mission San Diego de Alcalá was secularized in 1834. In 1846, the Mexican government gave the lands to Santiago Argüello, a local businessman. Soon the mission fell into ruins.

Mexico's hold on Alta California was short-lived. In the 1840s, American settlers in California petitioned the United States government to allow California to become a state. American troops began to fight the Mexicans for control of the land. In 1850, following a period of fighting, California became a U.S. state. Between 1853 and 1858, Mission San Diego de Alcalá was used by American troops as a base.

In the 1850s and 1860s, the United States Federal Land Commission sought to return the mission lands to the Roman Catholic Church. In 1862, President Abraham Lincoln signed a proclamation restoring 22 acres (8.9 hectares) of the original Mission San Diego de Alcalá complex to the Catholics.

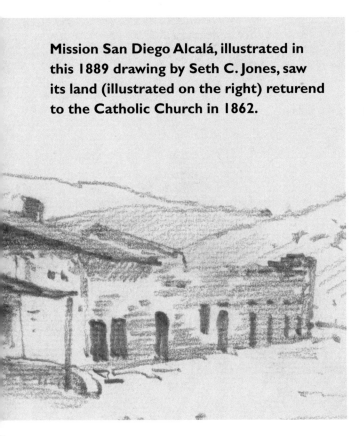

Mission San Diego Alcalá, illustrated in this 1889 drawing by Seth C. Jones, saw its land (illustrated on the right) returend to the Catholic Church in 1862.

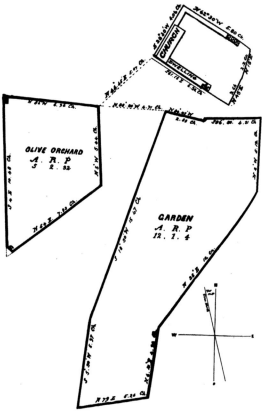

Today Mission San Diego has been restored and still serves the local community.

9 The Mission Today

In the latter part of the nineteenth and mid-twentieth centuries, Mission San Diego de Alcalá experienced revivals that would restore the mission into the beautiful site it is today.

RESTORING THE MISSION

In the 1890s, Fray Anthony Dominic Ubach began restoration efforts at Mission San Diego de Alcalá. Loved by many, he was a devout leader of the Catholic faith. He ministered to and advocated for the Native people in the region. By the time of Fray Ubach's arrival, only the entrance of the mission church remained standing. Fray Ubach saw the structure's crumbling state and decided to do something about it. Under his direction, a religious order of nuns built a school for Native children at the mission, which operated for seventeen years. Many of the mission buildings and artifacts, such as the mission bells, were restored over time under his guidance.

LEGACY OF THE MISSIONS

Now restored, Mission San Diego de Alcalá serves the community as a church and historical center. It is open to tourists year-round, and the church serves many families in the area. In the late 1960s,

Excavation at the mission grounds in the 1960s unearthed many artifacts from the mission that are now part of the Jaymé Museum and the mission's grounds.

Dr. Raymond Brandes, an archaeologist, and students from University of San Diego **excavated** the site, looking for original building foundations and artifacts. One of the main features discovered during that time, and now on display at the mission, are Fray Junípero Serra's living quarters. It has since been restored to its original condition. In 1976, the mission church was designated a Minor Basilica, a high honor from the Catholic Pope. Today the mission offers visitors the opportunity to view many artifacts in its Fray Jaymé Museum as well as on its grounds.

The legacy of agricultural production started by the missionaries has continued for more than two centuries, making California the most productive state in the U.S. The city of San Deigo, which was founded on the land surrounding San Diego de Alcalá, has grown into a booming city and is now the second most populous city in the largest state in the country. Today, the mission itself stands as a lasting testimony to the difficulties of building modern-day California, and of the lives and cultures that changed forever over the years. Mission San Diego de Alcalá, along with the twenty other missions, remains a lasting memory of the triumphs and hardships that form the history of California.

10
Make Your Own Mission Model

To make your own model of the San Diego de Alcalá mission, you will need:

- cardboard (brown)
- construction paper (red and green)
- glue
- masking tape
- miniature bells (5)
- miniature trees and flowers
- paint (reddish-brown)
- pencil
- penne pasta
- scissors
- toothpicks
- white cardboard

DIRECTIONS

Adult supervision is suggested.

Step 1: Cut a 22"× 16" (55.9 × 40.6 centimeters) piece of brown cardboard for the base of the mission complex.

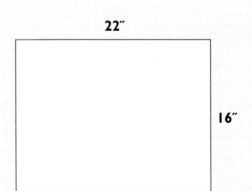

22"

16"

Step 2: To make the side walls for the friars' quarters, cut out two pieces of white cardboard measuring 16" × 3" (40.6 cm × 7.6 cm).

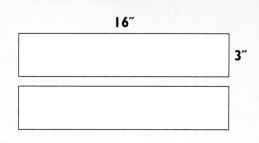

Step 3: Cut two pieces of white cardboard measuring 3½" × 5" (8.9 cm × 12.7 cm). Cut the corners off the top of each to form a pointed shape with 3" (7.6 cm) walls.

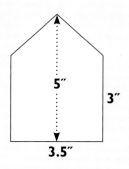

Step 4: Glue these four pieces together so they form a building. Tape the walls together at the corners.

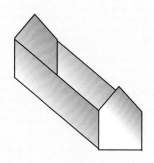

Step 5: Draw and then cut a rectangular shape from the cardboard measuring 12½" × 3" (31.8 cm × 7.6 cm). Glue it to one of the ends of the friars' quarters. Allow it to dry. This is the back wall of the quadrangle.

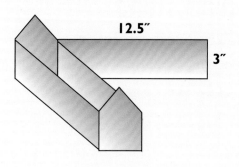

Step 6: Cut an 11" × 3" (27.9 × 7.6 cm) piece of cardboard. Tape it to the back wall so it forms the third side of the quadrangle.

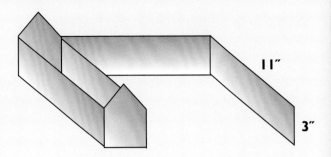

11"

3"

Step 7: To make the front of the church, cut a piece of cardboard measuring 8" × 9" (20.3 cm × 22.9 cm). Cut the top so that it has a wavy shape. Draw and then cut out a window.

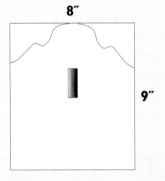

8"

9"

Step 8: To make the bell wall, cut a piece of cardboard measuring 4 ½" × 11" (11.4 cm × 27.9 cm). Cut the top so that it has a rounded tip.

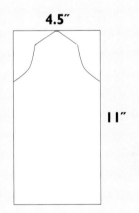

4.5"

11"

Step 9: In the bell wall, draw and cut out five openings for the bells. Slide the bells onto the toothpicks, and tape the toothpicks behind the openings.

Step 10: Tape the front of the church onto the edge of the quadrangle wall. Tape the bell wall next to it.

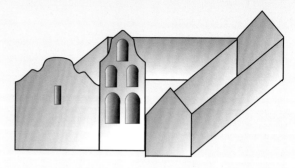

Step 11: For the roof of the friars' quarters, cut a piece of cardboard measuring 16" × 5½" (40.6 cm × 14 cm). Fold it in half lengthwise and glue it onto the building. Allow it to dry.

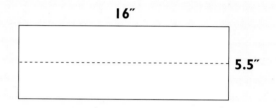

Step 12: Glue pieces of penne pasta on the roof in neat rows. Allow them to dry. Then paint the penne pasta reddish-brown.

Step 13: Draw and then cut a door for the church out of brown cardboard and glue it in place under the window. Allow it to dry.

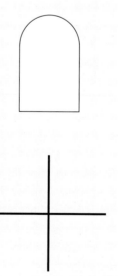

Step 14: Glue two toothpicks behind the church window so they form a cross.

Step 15: Glue red paper in front of the church and the bell wall. Glue green paper inside the courtyard. Add trees or flowers to decorate the mission grounds.

The model of Mission San Diego when it is completed.

Key Dates in Mission History

1492	Christopher Columbus reaches the West Indies
1542	Cabrillo's expedition to California
1602	Sebastián Vizcaíno sails to California
1713	Fray Junípero Serra is born
1769	Founding of San Diego de Alcalá
1770	Founding of San Carlos Borroméo del Río Carmelo
1771	Founding of San Antonio de Padua and San Gabriel Arcángel
1772	Founding of San Luis Obispo de Tolosa
1775–76	Founding of San Juan Capistrano
1776	Founding of San Francisco de Asís
1776	Declaration of Independence is signed

1777	Founding of Santa Clara de Asís
1782	Founding of San Buenaventura
1784	Fray Serra dies
1786	Founding of Santa Bárbara
1787	Founding of La Purísima Concepción
1791	Founding of Santa Cruz and Nuestra Señora de la Soledad
1797	Founding of San José, San Juan Bautista, San Miguel Arcángel, and San Fernando Rey de España
1798	Founding of San Luis Rey de Francia
1804	Founding of Santa Inés
1817	Founding of San Rafael Arcángel
1823	Founding of San Francisco Solano
1833	Mexico passes Secularization Act
1848	Gold found in northern California
1850	California becomes the thirty-first state

Glossary

adobe (uh-DOH-bee)
Brick made from dried mud and straw.

aqueduct (AH-kwuh-dukt)
A manmade ditch that carries water from its source to another source, usually over long distances.

convert (kuhn-VERT)
To change religious beliefs.

excavate (EX-kuh-vay-t)
To uncover ancient ruins and find artifacts from the past.

feast day (FEE-st day)
A day in the Catholic religious group that celebrates a particular saint.

hide (HYD)
The skin of an animal.

irrigation system (eer-ih-GEY-shun sis-tem)
Manmade pathways from a water source to a location meant to water an area.

neophyte (NEE-oh-fyt)
A person who has converted to another religion.

quadrangle (KWAH-drayn-gul) The square at the center of a mission that is surrounded by four buildings.

ritual (RIH-choo-uhl)
Something done as part of a formal or religious ceremony.

secularization (sehk-yoo-luh-rih-ZAY-shun) Turning over the operation of the mission lands to the Native Americans.

thatch (THACH) Twigs, grass, and bark bundled together.

Pronunciation Guide

atole (ah-TOH-lay)

campanario (kam-pan-NAH-ree-oh)

carretas (kah-RAY-tahs)

fray (FRAY)

Kumeyaay (KOOM-yaay)

pozole (poh-SOH-lay)

siesta (see-EHS-tah)

Find Out More

To learn more about the California missions, check out these books and websites.

BOOKS

Gray-Kanatiiosh, Barbara A. *Kumeyaay*. Edina, MN: ABDO, 2006.

Hackel, Stephen W. *Junípero Serra: California's Founding Father*. New York, NY: Hill and Wang, 2013.

Leffingwell, Randy, and Alastair Worden. *California Missions and Presidios*. St. Paul, MN: Voyageur Press, 2005.

Young, Stanley, Melba Levick, and Sally B. Woodbridge. *The Missions of California*. San Francisco, CA: Chronicle Books, 2004.

WEBSITES

California History & Culture Conservancy

www.historyandculture.com/chcc/presidio1.html

Take a photographic tour and explore Presidio Park today and compare it to its past. Discover the West Coast's first military encampment and learn how the Spanish empire established a stronghold which later became the city of San Diego.

California Missions Foundation

www.californiamissionsfoundation.org

Explore El Camino Real's trail from San Diego to Sonoma while learning about the oldest surviving structures in the state of California.

California Missions Resource Center

www.missionscalifornia.com

Take advantage of this comprehensive and unique resource and discover historical information on the twenty-one California missions. Learn about key dates and major events.

Kumeyaay History

www.kumeyaay.info/history

Discover evidence that the Kumeyaay have lived in the greater San Diego and northern Baja California Mexico area for some 12,000 years. View photos and follow links to other historic San Diego sites.

Official Website of Mission San Diego de Alcalá

www.missionsandiego.com

Learn more about Mission San Diego de Alcalá's history, view detailed photographs, or book a tour of the mission.

Index